Secrets Of Effective Leadership For IT Managers

Tips And Techniques That IT Managers Can Use In Order To Develop Leadership Skills

"Practical, proven techniques that will help you to manage your IT Manager career successfully"

Dr. Jim Anderson

Published by:
Blue Elephant Consulting
Tampa, Florida

Copyright © 2013 by Dr. Jim Anderson

All rights reserved. No part of this book may be reproduced of transmitted in any form or by any means, electronic or mechanical, including photocopying, recording or by any information storage and retrieval system without written permission of the publisher, except for inclusion of brief quotations in a review.

Printed in the United States of America

Library of Congress Control Number: 2013922140

ISBN-13: 978-1494325756

ISBN-10: 1494325756

Warning – Disclaimer

The purpose of this book is to educate and entertain. This book does not promise or guarantee that anyone following the ideas, tips, suggestions, techniques or strategies will be successful. The author, publisher and distributor(s) shall have neither liability nor responsibility to anyone with respect to any loss or damage caused, or alleged to be caused, directly or indirectly by the information contained in this book.

Recent Books By The Author

Product Management

- How To Have A Successful Product Manager Career: The Things That You Need To Be Doing TODAY In Order To Have A Successful Product Manager Career

- Product Manager Product Success: How to keep your product on track and make it become a success

- Communication Skills For Product Managers: The Communication Skills That Product Managers Need To Know How To Use In Order To Have A Successful Product

- Customer Lessons For Product Managers: Techniques For Product Managers To Better Understand What Their Customers Really Want

Public Speaking

- Secrets To Planning The Perfect Speech

- Secrets To Organizing The Perfect Speech: How to organize the best speech of your life!

- Secrets To Creating The Perfect Speech: How to create a speech that will make your message be remembered forever!

- How To Rehearse In Order To Give The Perfect Speech: How to effectively rehearse your next speech to that your message be remembered forever!

CIO Skills

- Managing Your CIO Career: Steps That CIOs Have To Take In Order To Have A Long And Successful Career

- CIO Communication Skills Secrets: Tips And Techniques For CIOs To Use In Order To Become Better Communicators

- How CIOs Can Make Innovation Happen: Tips And Techniques For CIOs To Use In Order To Make Innovation Happen In Their IT Department

IT Manager Skills

- IT Manager Budgeting Skills

- IT Manager Career Secrets: Tips And Techniques That IT Managers Can Use In Order To Have A Successful Career

Negotiating

- Preparing For Your Next Negotiation: What You Need To Do BEFORE A Negotiation Starts In Order To Get The Best Possible Deal

- How To Open Your Next Negotiation: How To Start A Negotiation In Order To Get The Best Possible Outcome

Note: See a complete list of books by Dr. Jim Anderson at the back of this book.

Acknowledgements

Any book like this one is the result of years of real-world work experience. In my over 25 years of working for 7 different firms, I have met countless fantastic people and I've been mentored by some truly exceptional ones. Although I've probably forgotten some of the people who made me the person that I am today, here is my attempt to finally give them the recognition that they so truly deserve:

- Thomas P. Anderson
- Art Puett
- Bobbi Marshall
- Bob Boggs

Dr. Jim Anderson

This book is dedicated to my wife Lori. None of this would have been possible without her love and support.

Thanks for the best 21 years of my life (so far)...!

Table Of Contents

LEARNING TO LEAD EFFECTIVELY 8

ABOUT THE AUTHOR 10

CHAPTER 1: FIX IT & FORGET IT? NOPE, DOESN'T WORK FOR IT 15

CHAPTER 2: 4 DRIVERS OF EMPLOYEE MOTIVATION THAT ALL IT LEADERS MUST KNOW 18

CHAPTER 3: IT LEADERS' SECRET TECHNIQUES FOR MOTIVATING STAFF 21

CHAPTER 4: IT LEADERS HAVE TWO OF THESE BUT DO THEY USE THEM? 24

CHAPTER 5: WHAT CAN COOL DESIGN FIRMS TEACH IT MANAGERS? 28

CHAPTER 6: HOW CAN A MANAGER MANAGE IT WORKERS WHEN THERE IS NO COMPANY LOYALTY? 31

CHAPTER 7: ARE YOU A SOCIALLY INTELLIGENT IT LEADER? 34

CHAPTER 8: MIRROR, MIRROR ON THE WALL, WHO'S THE BEST IT MANAGER OF ALL? 37

CHAPTER 9: ARE YOU A "TUNED IN" IT MANAGER? 40

CHAPTER 10: SIMPLE STEPS TO BECOMING A BETTER IT MANAGER.43

CHAPTER 11: 3 IT MANAGER SECRETS FROM THE FOLKS AT PIXAR ..46

CHAPTER 12: IT MANAGER BREAKTHROUGHS: THE POWER OF A PEER CULTURE 49

Learning To Lead Effectively

Anyone can manage IT employees. Due to the fact that the employees have agreed to work for the company, as their manager you hold the ability to fire them in your hands. If they don't do what you tell them to do, you have the right to terminate them. That's management, not leadership.

Leadership has to do with getting your IT team to WANT to do what you need them to do. When you are leading your team, when you are not around they continue to work towards the goals that you have established for the team because they believe in the goals and in you. Leadership is much more powerful than management.

Leadership is also much harder to learn how to do. It has a great deal to do with understanding what motivates the members of your team and then finding ways to associate the team's goals with what each member of the team is trying to accomplish in both their career and in their personal life.

Examples of how to be a better leader can be found in many different places. Not all of these examples come from within IT. As an IT manager you need to learn how to keep your eyes open so that you can spot and learn from the good examples of leadership that are all around us each and every day.

Understanding the various members of your team is a key part of knowing how best to lead them. This requires you to be socially intelligent and to have the ability to be "tuned in" to their needs.

This book will provide you with numerous examples of good leadership. I'll be showing you the skills and talents that IT leaders must have in order to do a good job of motivating their team. Creating a culture of leadership will allow your team to achieve more using the resources that are available to you.

For more information on what it takes to be a great IT manager, check out my blog, The Accidental IT Leader, at:

www.TheAccidentalITLeader.com

Good luck!

- Dr. Jim Anderson

About The Author

I must confess that I never set out to be a CIO. When I went to school, I studied Computer Science and thought that I'd get a nice job programming and that would be that. Well, at least part of that plan worked out!

My first job was working for Boeing on their F/A-18 fighter jet program. I spent my days programming fighter jet software in assembly language and I loved it. The U.S. government decided to save some money and went looking for other countries to sell this plane to. This put me into an unfamiliar role: I started to meet with foreign military officials and I ended up having to manage groups of engineers who were working on international projects.

Time moved on and so did I. I found myself working for Siemens, the big German telecommunications company. They were making phone switches and selling them to the seven U.S. phone companies. The problem was that the switches were too complicated. Customers couldn't tell the difference between one complicated phone switch from another complicated phone switch. Once again I found myself working with the sales and marketing teams to find ways to make the great technology that the engineers had developed understandable to both internal and external customers.

I've spent over 25 years working as an senior IT professional for both big companies and startups. This has given me an opportunity to learn what it takes to manage and IT department in ways that allow it to maximize its output while becoming a valuable part of the overall company.

I now live in Tampa Florida where I spend my time managing my consulting business, Blue Elephant Consulting, teaching college courses at the University of South Florida, and traveling to work with companies like yours to share the knowledge that I have about how to create and manage successful IT departments.

I'm always available to answer questions and I can be reached at:

Dr. Jim Anderson
Blue Elephant Consulting
Email: jim@BlueElephantConsulting.com
Facebook: http://goo.gl/1TVoK
Web: **www.BlueElephantConsulting.com**

"Unforgettable communication skills that will set your ideas free..."

Create IT Departments That Are Productive And A Valuable Asset To The Rest Of The Company !

Dr. Jim Anderson is available to provide training and coaching on the topics that are the most important to people who have to manage IT departments: how can I build a productive IT department (and keep it together) while at the same time providing the rest of the company with the IT services that they need?

Dr. Anderson believes that in order to both learn and remember what he says, speakers need to laugh. Each one of his speeches is full of fun and humor so that what he says "sticks" with everyone.

Dr. Anderson's CIO SkillsTraining Includes:

1. How to identify and attract the right type of IT workers to your IT department.
2. How to build relationships with the company's senior management in order to get the support that you need?
3. How to stay on top of changing technology and security issues so that you never get surprised?

Dr. Jim Anderson works with over 100 customers per year. To invite Dr. Anderson to work with you, contact him at:

Phone: 813-418-6970 or
Email: jim@BlueElephantConsulting.com

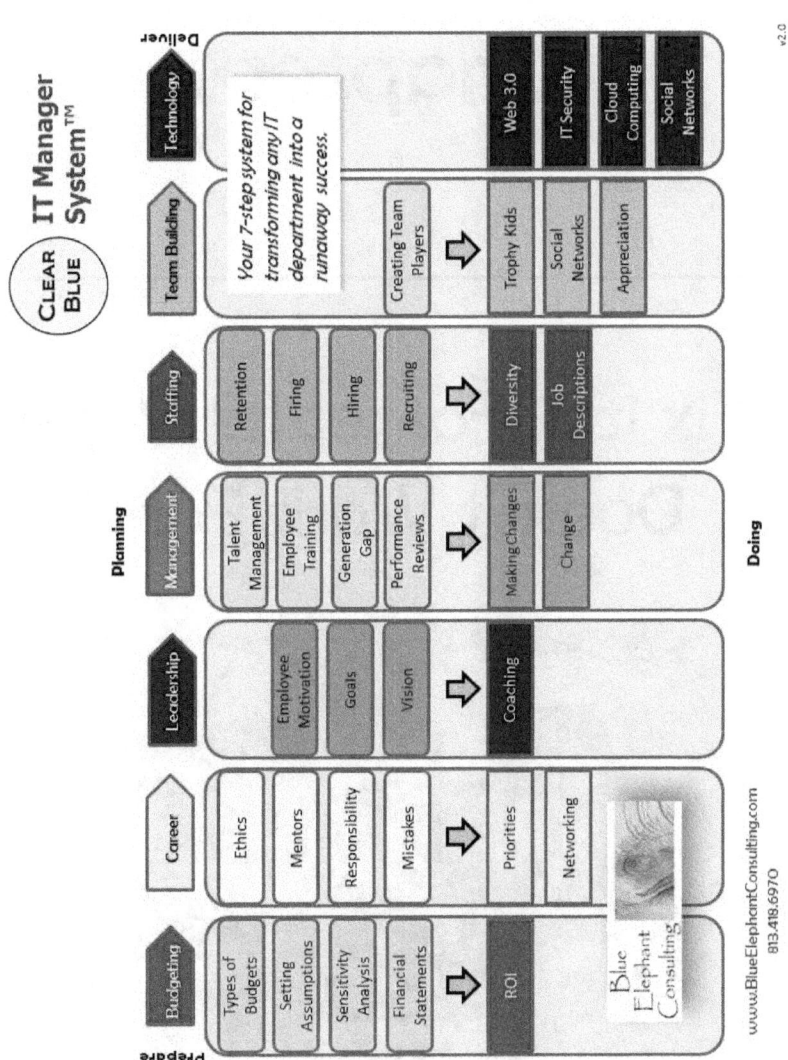

The **Clear Blue IT Manager System™** has been created to provide IT managers with a clear roadmap for how to manage an IT team. This system shows IT Managers what needs to be done and in what order to do it.

Chapter 1

Fix It & Forget It? Nope, Doesn't Work For IT

Chapter 1: Fix It & Forget It? Nope, Doesn't Work For IT

If, like me, you actually enjoy reading the 100+ business books that get published every year then you are probably well aware of what I like to call "the silver bullet syndrome". In any given business book, the author generally describes a problem, documents the approaches that had been tried to solve the problem, and then finally gets around to describing the solution that finally saved the day.

You can pick your favorite management strategy: TQM, Black Belt, Just In Time, etc. and there are multiple books that basically tell the same story.

That's why when I was leafing through the Theory & Practice section of the Wall Street Journal, my attention was caught by an article by Phred Dvorak titled **"Experts Have a Message for Managers: Shake It Up"**. The gist of the article was that management practices that solve a particular problem at a given point in time can eventually turn on a team. This has some significant impacts for IT teams.

The article goes on to say that if you keep doing the same things over and over, even if they made you a great team at one point in time, then they will eventually lead to problems. The reasons for this dire eventuality are because you can develop tunnel vision, start to resist new ideas, stop experimenting, start to build silos, and stop being able to adapt to new changes. Dang — I thought that if I could only find & read the right book, then all of my problems would be solved.

It turns out that the experts recommend that in order for an IT team to succeed in the long term, you need to set up processes & procedures that naturally cause tension and collaboration at the same time. Having both of these conditions present at the same time will help keep the team open and able to change. You have to be careful to manage both of these — too much of either will result in a workplace that nobody wants to be a part of.

Ok you say, so how can this be done on my IT team? You have many choices: reorganizing the team is a quick and dirty way to shake things up quickly. How about telling everyone that their job descriptions are only temporary. There is the IT classic: give different team members different goals (reduce costs, produce twice as many products). Separating tasks and making team members dependent on each other in order to complete projects will also introduce new challenges.

At the end of the day I guess we are all just a little bit like zoo animals. We can get very used to what works when it is working well. We say that friction is bad, but it turns out that we all need just a little bit of conflict in our lives in order to keep us engaged in what we are doing.

Chapter 2

4 Drivers Of Employee Motivation That All IT Leaders Must Know

Chapter 2: 4 Drivers Of Employee Motivation That All IT Leaders Must Know

We've talked about the fact that sometimes employee motivation can be a lot like performing brain surgery – you've got to be careful or you'll end up doing a lot of damage. If an IT manager can realize that their staff (indeed all humans) have four fundamental emotional drivers that need to be met, then they are well on their way to maximizing employee satisfaction and maximizing productivity.

So what are these four drivers that we all respond to?

- **The Drive To Acquire:** More! More! More! As human beings we are all programmed to go out and get scarce goods (iPhone?) that make us feel better about ourselves. I think that we can all agree that we feel "happy" when we are successful and we feel "sad" when we fail.

    It's not just physical things that we desire, but also experiences and improvements in our social status. This drive is relative – we are always comparing what we have to what those around us have. Oh, and it's insatiable – we always want more, more, more!

- **The Drive To Bond:** We all know about how we bond with our parents, siblings, etc. However, the human creature is amazing because we have the additional ability to extend who we bond with to associations, organizations, and even countries.

    This is a big one – when we are successful in bonding, then we fell loved. When we are not successful in bonding, then we feel loneliness. For your IT workers, bonding at work is a critical part of who they are.

When staff feel proud to be part of an organization (Starbucks?) this can be a big boost to their motivation. It also explains why we get so depressed when we get fired or laid off – we feel that the organization has betrayed us.

- **The Drive To Comprehend:** We are creatures that really want to understand the world in which we live. We are constantly using scientific, cultural, and even religious theories to try to make sense of it all.

  Our reason for doing this is that we want to be able to come up with reasonable responses to things that happen in our environment and to be able to determine what actions we should take next.

- **The Drive To Defend:** You knew that this one had to be on the list! When external threats show up, we humans naturally defend ourselves, our family & friends, our property and things, etc.

  Remember that "fight" thing? Fulfilling this drive leads employees to feel secure, failing to fulfill it leads to strong emotions like fear and resentment. This drive is one reason why mergers or buyouts can be so devastating for staff.

Now that you know what the four drivers of your staff are, the big question is what is the best way to use these drivers to make sure that the members of your team are motivated to work hard?

Chapter 3

IT Leaders' Secret Techniques For Motivating Staff

Chapter 3: IT Leaders' Secret Techniques For Motivating Staff

Now that we've discovered that all humans, including those in in your IT department / on your IT team, respond to four basic drives, we are now faced with the really big question: how does an IT leader use this knowledge to motivate his/her staff? It turns out that there are actually a number of possible levers that you can pull...

The Drive To Acquire Is Handled By How You Handle Rewards: This is, of course, a classic staff driving lever. How well your IT department sorts out the good performers from the poor ones, how it matches the rewards that it hands out to performance delivered, and how easily it permits talented staff to advance in the organization determines how well you are meeting your employee's drive to acquire.

The Drive To Bond Is Handled By Your Department's Culture: Put simply, this comes down to how much camaraderie exists within the department. Does your staff work well together? Is there openness, teamwork, and genuine friendship among the people who work for you?

The Drive To Comprehend Is Handled By How You Design Jobs: Are the IT jobs in your department both meaningful, interesting, while at the same time challenging? These are all critical to meeting the needs of this drive.

The Drive To Defend Is Handled By Your Performance Review Process: If the annual performance review process is seen as being fair and trustworthy by all, and if resources are allocated in a transparent way then this will meet your staff's drive to defend.

The key take-away for you regarding all of this drive stuff, is that in survey after survey, IT employees reported that when there was even a small enhancement to their ability to fulfill any one of these four drives, then their overall motivation shot up.

However, (this is also a key point) all four drives have to be met – missing even one can significantly dampen an employee's motivation.

Finally, employees have said that the statements and actions that their immediate IT managers make are just as important to their overall productivity as all of the company's policies and rules. Now that's something for IT leaders to spend some time thinking about...!

Chapter 4

IT Leaders Have Two Of These But Do They Use Them?

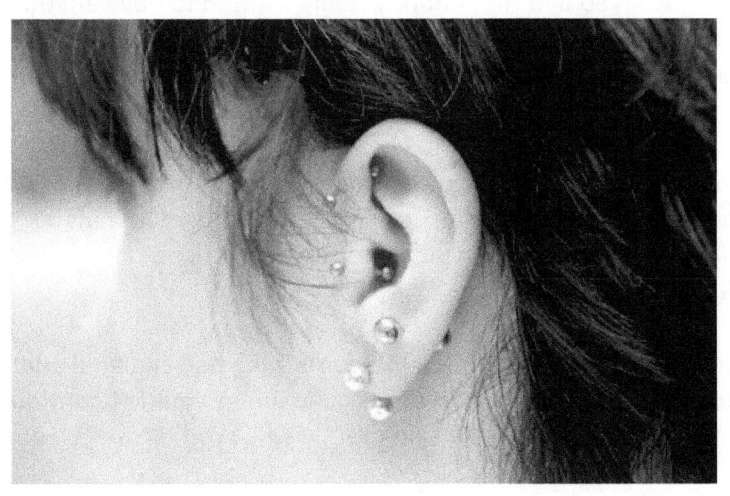

Chapter 4: IT Leaders Have Two Of These But Do They Use Them?

About a year ago I had a chance to sit down with a member of an IT team that was working for me in order to have a heart-to-heart with him. We'll call him Tim.

Tim was a project manager on one of my teams and so far he had been a steady performer. I'd say that he was strong on the analytical side and soft on the interpersonal side; however, he was doing a good job and I had really had no complaints on his performance.

Recently, things had changed with Tim. His whole demeanor had been transformed as a deep depression seemed to both surround him and flow off of him and onto anyone that he interacted with.

It had gotten so bad that nobody really wanted to have anything to do with him. Clearly this was having an impact on his ability to do his job. It was time for me to step in and see what I could do.

I took Tim with me down to the cafeteria in order to get him into a neutral location. I started my conversation with him by explaining that I had been pleased with his work up until recently.

I told him that it sure seemed like something had changed and I needed to find out what it was because things couldn't continue like they were. Tim initially said exactly what you'd expect a guy to say: "Nothing's wrong."

I thought about opening up on him with both barrels – look, he was doing a lousy job and he was going to be out the door if he didn't shape up. However, I knew better and so I kept gently probing.

Finally, Tim got around to saying "I hate my Director." Once again, my gut reaction was to tell him "Too bad, he's not leaving so you had better make some changes." However, somehow I was able to hold my tongue and instead said the three most important words that an IT Leader can say "Tell Me More…"

Tim started telling me the standard things that everyone says about their boss behind their backs. "He doesn't give clear instructions, he changes his mind too often, he's never around when I need to talk to him, etc."

This is regular stuff – not enough to cause such a change in personality. So I went on and said "What else has happened lately?" This finally got Tim to confess everything.

In a staff meeting, his boss had found some errors in some slides that Tim had prepared showing the status of the project and had called him out on it in front of the rest of the department. Given Tim's personality, this was just about the worst thing that anyone could do to him. He was wounded and still sulking several weeks after the event. Bingo! We had our smoking gun.

This was a problem that I could (and did) fix rather easily. That's not the point of this chapter. Rather, my first reactions as Tim's story unfolded would have been the wrong ones to act on and if I had, then I would have ended up doing a great deal of damage and not fixing the problem. I guess that's why we all have two ears and just one mouth.

David Benzel is an author and a speaker and he points out that as IT Leaders we all have four main responsibilities when it comes to communicating with our IT teams:

1. To listen
2. To get the facts
3. To determine the problem
4. To help resolve the situation

As hard as it is to do, listening is both an art and a science that all of us IT Leaders need to get better at doing. Listening is hard to do because it requires you to focus your attention and use your full brain to process what is being said – no multi-tasking allowed!

By keeping your mouth shut and your ears open, you allow your staff to do the talking and when they do that, you will learn amazing things.

Chapter 5

What Can Cool Design Firms Teach IT Managers?

Chapter 5: What Can Cool Design Firms Teach IT Managers?

Each and every IT manager has problems. These problems run from the simple ("How can I meet that deadline") to the more complex ("These people don't like each other, how can I get them to work as a team?").

Sometimes we run into problems that despite our deep belief in ourselves, we just don't seem to be able to solve. What to do then?

I'm afraid that all too often we have a habit of just letting the problem linger. We believe that we are the only ones who will eventually be able to solve it and so we just let the problem sit there because we think that we'll eventually be able to dream up a way to solve it someday.

Well guess what, that's probably not going to happen. Some innovative firms are doing something about this problem – they are reaching out to those really cool design firms that you are always reading about and asking for management help.

One great example of this was reported on by Phred Dvorak in the Wall Street Journal. Dvorak found out that the extremely cool design firm IDEO (they came up with the concept for Apple's first mouse and apparently also the first soft-handled toothbrush) was contacted by the Sloan-Kettering Cancer Center to help find ways to make chemotherapy easier on patients.

Instead of doing what pretty much any IT manager would do – which is to document and study the process of treating patients, the kids at IDEO instead decided to look at the process from the patient's point-of-view. The IDEO team had Sloan-Kettering staff follow patients from their home to the clinic and then all the way through their treatment.

Before IDEO had been brought in, the Sloan-Kettering folks had naturally assumed that waiting time was the biggest deal to their patients and had been trying a bunch of tweaks to reduce it. It turns out that they were wrong.

The IDEO team discovered that there is another step in the process that caused more concern than all the waiting time in the world. There is a test that patients need to take in order to find out if they are strong enough to be treated on a given day.

Waiting for the results of that test is what really concerned their patients. When the clinic started offering this test the day before the treatment so that patients would know if they really were going to be treated, then customer satisfaction soared.

So what does all of this cancer treatment stuff have to do with IT leadership? Simple, the IDEO team has a great deal to teach us about solving people problems.

We love technology and we often feel that if we have enough metrics than we can solve any problem. However, sometimes what is really called for is for us to stop playing ourselves and instead start to play the role of our staff and our customers.

Taking the time to see the world from their point-of-view and understanding the constraints that they are living with can go a long way towards helping us to find new and innovative ways of solving those problems that have been lingering for far too long.

Chapter 6

How Can A Manager Manage IT Workers When There Is No Company Loyalty?

Chapter 6: How Can A Manager Manage IT Workers When There Is No Company Loyalty?

Welcome to the 21st Century where all IT workers now view themselves as temporary workers. The constant cycles of downsizing and outsourcing have made even the most committed workers view their jobs as being not so much as a career, but rather as a temporary pit-stop.

Add to this situation the arrival of the young Generation Y workers and all of a sudden an IT manager has a situation on his/her hands that they were never trained to handle. Put all of these factors together and suddenly company loyalty is a thing of the past.

The way that IT employees used to move forward is also something that is going out the door. Gen Y IT workers are actively looking for career paths that have shorter steps.

What this means for IT managers is that they need to find ways to understand what the expectations of their team members are. Once this is known, the manager will need to make sure that opportunities to gain experience are made available.

As though this was not complicated enough, an IT manager needs to be careful. There are also lots of IT employees who have been working their way up the career ladder using the traditional route and they are not going to be happy if others start moving up quicker than they did.

One thing that may help IT managers is that their companies are also changing. We are starting to see companies moving away from the traditional seniority-based IT career paths and are now starting to focus more on employee performance and future potential. This can mix things up as good workers of all ages start to move up through the ranks.

The tools that are used in the IT workplace reflect the new reality of the office. Face-to-face contact is going by the wayside more and more often.

This is due to work groups that are spread out and workloads that seem to be always increasing. Just like phone conferences replaced fact-to-face meetings, emails replaced phone conferences, now IM and texting are replacing emails.

It turns out that loyalty still exists in IT departments – it's just no longer given to the company. A great IT leader or a project that has real merit will capture the attention of jaded IT workers as well as Gen Y workers.

IT managers who can clearly communicate a driving purpose for the work that is being done will always attract the best and the brightest workers. No company loyalty required.

Chapter 7

Are You A Socially Intelligent IT Leader?

Chapter 7: Are You A Socially Intelligent IT Leader?

Them thar brain researchers are at it again. This time around they've been doing research in the field of social neuroscience. This is where they study what happens in your brain when you interact with other people. Oh oh! They are starting to get a handle on what it takes to make a good IT leader...

Daniel Goleman and Richard Boyatzis have written an article in the Harvard Business Review in which they lay out these findings. Keep in mind that Goleman is the one who wrote the hugely popular book **Social Intelligence: The New Science of Human Relationships**.

One of the key discoveries to come out of this research is that it's the things that IT leaders do that can affect both their own brain chemistry as well as the brain chemistry of those who work for them. These things include tuning in to other people's moods as well as showing empathy.

What researchers are finding is that it's not correct to say that a great IT leader's mind is operating by itself. Rather what seems to be happening is that IT leaders' minds' are "fusing" with the minds of the people that they are leading. The really great IT leaders are the ones who can make the best use of this single fused mind.

What this is all leading to is that it turns out that the way to become a better IT leader is for you to find authentic work contexts in which you will be able to reinforce this type of brain fusing.

To take this one step further, being a good leader is much less about being good at handling specific situations.

Instead, what is important is that you learn how to develop an interest in the people who work for you / with you and find ways to create positive feelings in these same people.

So what is this "**social intelligence**" thing? Goleman and Boyatzis define it as being "*a set of interpersonal competencies built on specific neural circuits ... that inspire others to be effective*". Oh, it's brain stuff.

We've all known smart people who were really bad leaders. The two sets of skills do not always go hand-in-hand. What researchers are starting to understand is that the social skills that are needed to be a good IT leader may actually have a biological basis.

If you know and understand this linkage, then you can change your behavior and state to reinforce the neural links between you and your team.

Chapter 8

Mirror, Mirror On The Wall, Who's The Best IT Manager Of All?

Chapter 8: Mirror, Mirror On The Wall, Who's The Best IT Manager Of All?

Those boys who get locked up and do work on behavior neuroscience continue to come up with new and interesting discoveries all the time. This time around they've made a stunning discovery that will have a long lasting impact on how IT managers do their job. Do I have your interest yet?

Daniel Goleman and Richard Boyatzis have written an article in the Harvard Business Review in which they describe what's been going on in the world of neuroscience. Neuroscientists have discovered something called "**mirror neurons**" that are spread out all over our brains. Our brains have lots and lots of neurons. This newly discovered type appear to mimic (or "mirror") what someone else is doing.

These neurons were discovered by Italian neuroscientists who were studying one particular type of cell in a monkey's brain. This cell only fired when the monkey raised its arm. One day an assistant in the lab raised some food to his mouth and the cell in the monkey fired.

What this all means is that when we detect someone's (consciously or unconsciously) emotions by observing their actions, these newly discovered mirror neurons reproduce the emotions that we believe that they are feeling. Taken all together, these neurons allow us to create a virtually instant sense of having a shared experience.

Why do we care about all of this brain stuff? It's the key to being a great IT leader. It turns out that your emotions and your actions are what your department / team are going to be mirroring. If you can activate the mirror neurons in those who are following you, then you will have tapped into a very powerful force.

Additional studies that have been done on groups to measure the effects of activating these neurons have revealed even more. It turns out that when you are addressing your department / team, HOW you communicate is much more important than WHAT you communicate.

This means that if you want to get the best performance out of your team, you need to be demanding (of course) but do in in such a way that creates a happy positive mood in your team. This is all based on the simple fact that when your people feel better, then you'll get better performance out of them.

Which now brings us to the subject of laughter. I'm not talking about having your team laugh at you (they may already be doing this). Instead, I'm talking about how often you get your team to laugh **with** you. Studies have shown that the best IT leaders got their employees to laugh on average three times as often as did midperforming IT leaders.

When you are in a good mood, this helps the people who work with and for you to both take in the information that you are providing as well as react quicker and with more creativity.

Chapter 9

Employee Motivation: Are You A "Tuned In" IT Manager?

Chapter 9: Are You A "Tuned In" IT Manager?

Just how do great IT managers go about making decisions? We all have different ways of doing this, but many of us talk about making "gut decisions". What this is really a way of saying is that an IT leader who has good business instincts is a great value to the company that they work for.

Daniel Goleman and Richard Boyatzis have written an article in the Harvard Business Review in which they call this type of leadership as being the ability to recognize patterns. We'd all like to have more of this kind of accurate decision making ability – so where does it come from? Bad news here – it comes from extensive experience.

If you want to become known as someone who can make good, quick decisions, then start trusting your gut; however, also make sure that you get as many inputs from others as possible. The time that it requires to get inputs from others can often take too long to collect. What's an IT leader to do?

It turns out that you can probably trust your gut. This is because in your brain you have a class of neuron cells that are called "**spindle cells**". This type of neuron both attaches to other cells easier and transmits information to them quicker.

The ability to quickly connect and transmit judgments, beliefs, and emotions creates what scientists like to call our "social guidance system". This system gets used whenever we have to make a choice among several different alternatives.

This system also helps us to make up our minds as to if someone that we meet is trustworthy. It turns out that within 1/20th of a second these spindle cells will fire and we'll decide how we feel about someone. Studies have shown that these quick decisions actually turn out to be quite accurate.

What all this means is that as long as you can "tune in" to your staff's moods, you should feel comfortable trusting your gut instincts. There is a physical side to all of this that can impact your staff.

It's called "**resonance**". Researcher Annie McKee says that this is similar to what you see when you see people dancing together, getting ready to kiss, or when they are playing musical instruments together. Teams that are being led by a skilled IT leader are often physically coordinated in how and when their bodies move together during meetings.

Give this some thought and start trusting your gut more. It appears as though your first thought is more often than not the right decision!

Chapter 10

Simple Steps To Becoming A Better IT Manager

Chapter 10: Simple Steps To Becoming A Better IT Manager

A question that I often get asked by both new and old IT leaders is "how can I become a better manager?" The question is a simple one that has complex answers. What all IT leaders want is to become one of those leaders who has the ability to get all of our employees to light up when we show up. We want to be able to get them excited about us and about their jobs. How hard could that be?

Bad news here, it's actually fairly difficult to transform yourself into one of those very charismatic leaders if you are not already one. If you can't cause staff to naturally respond to you, then sometimes we try to make self-conscious efforts to display leadership traits. This can backfire on you and it can come across as forced. This is not going to get you where you want to be.

Daniel Goleman and Richard Boyatzis have written an article in the Harvard Business Review in which they report that if you really want to become a better IT leader, then you are going to have to undertake the hard work of actually changing your behavior.

What these researchers are really talking about is that to really break through what is holding you back as an IT manager, you are going to have to become socially smarter. We're not talking about MBA book knowledge here, but rather learning to interact with people better.

As an example of this, consider the case of a manager who just didn't know when to back off on an issue. She received feedback that this was her problem and she made several social changes. First she started anticipating how people would react to her. Next, she came up with different ways to present her opinion or information in a way that would not be so aggressive. Finally, she came up with a program that would allow her to change.

Another good way to develop the social skills that you need as an IT manager is to spend time with an IT leader who does a good job of managing. What will happen is that your brain will start to mirror what this leader is doing and this will allow you to become a better leader.

It's important for you to realize that your brain is constantly creating new neural networks. This means that the way you are is not the way that you will be. You are not a prisoner of your genes or previous management experiences. You can change and improve if you are willing to put the time and energy in to do so.

One final note, developing the social skills that you need to be a great IT leader is especially important when a crisis situation arises. Business conditions like a takeover, merger, or even layoffs can create a great deal of stress among IT workers. IT Leaders who have good social skills can keep the team together and get high performance out of them even during times like this.

Chapter 11

3 IT Manager Secrets From The Folks At Pixar

Chapter 11: 3 IT Manager Secrets From The Folks At Pixar

Toy Story, Cars, Finding Nemo, Wall-E – who hasn't been amazed at the movies that Pixar has created over the past few years? I think that we can all agree that clearly Pixar has found a way to foster and grow creativity within their organization. What if IT Leaders could find out how to do the same for our departments and teams...

Ed Catmull is one of the founders of Pixar and he is currently the president of Pixar and Disney Animation Studios (they merged just a while ago). He wrote an article for the Harvard Business Review in which he discussed just what makes Pixar work so well.

Catmull make the point that he was once talking with a studio executive who lamented the fact that his biggest problem was not finding good people, but rather finding good ideas.

Catmull flat out disagrees with this thinking – he thinks that it reflects a misunderstanding of creativity. He also thinks that it places way too much importance on the initial idea in creating a new product.

Since the release of Toy Story in 1995, Pixar has released eight other films which have all been blockbusters. The real interesting point is that Pixar has never bought a script or movie idea from the outside. The ingredients that make their movies magic, the stories, the characters, and the worlds in which they live, have all been created internally by Pixar employees.

Here's where the real learning for IT Leaders comes:

Catmull believes that Pixar's adherence to a basic set of principles and ways of managing creative talent and risk is done responsibly. At Pixar, the job of management is NOT to prevent risk but rather to build in the capability to recover when failures occur (and, of course, they do occur).

In order for this type of environment to exist, it must be safe to tell the truth. In order for the organization to grow and improve, it must constantly challenge all of its assumptions and be searching for any flaws that might destroy the organization.

IT Leaders, just like Pixar management, need to find a way to resist our built-in tendencies to try to either avoid or at least minimize risks. I realize that this is easy to say, and very hard to do.

If an IT Leader can't overcome his/her desire to avoid risk, then each project that they are in charge of will be an imperfect copy of a previous project that they worked on. This will result in many copies of what was never a perfect process with no hope of achieving a break through.

To have a breakthrough in how a project is done, IT Leaders need to be able to find a way to live with uncertainty. This of course means that you also need to make sure that your department or team has the built-in ability to recover when you've taken a big risk and it ends up failing.

Chapter 12

IT Manager Breakthroughs: The Power Of A Peer Culture

Chapter 12: IT Manager Breakthroughs: The Power Of A Peer Culture

So where should creativity live in an IT department? We use creativity to solve problems, create designs, and to determine what projects to pursue. IT Managers need to be the ones who have creative control within the IT department in order to ensure that projects get done correctly. However, this is often easier said than done...

Ed Catmull is one of the founders of Pixar and he is currently the president of Pixar and Disney Animation Studios (they merged just a while ago). He wrote an article for the Harvard Business Review in which he discussed how Pixar has learned to deal with managing all that creativity.

As an IT manager, your job is to get creative IT people on a team, make their task very clear to them, bet on them big time, ensure that they have a way to get honest feedback, and then give them a lot of leeway to make decisions and the support that they'll need to keep on going.

If that wasn't enough to make an IT Leader's job difficult, then the next part should just about do it. As an IT Leader, one of your main jobs is to observe your team.

What you are looking for is how they work to solve problems and if they are able to make progress. In essence, you are trying to observe the social dynamics that are in play within the team – no changes needed if everything is working. It's when it's not working that things start to get fun...

Catmull has seen his share of both successful and unsuccessful leaders. He points out that he believes that good leaders, of course, have great analytical skills.

However, he goes farther and says that they also have to be able to find a way to harness the analytical skills and work experience of those people who are on the team. I guess that's the difference between an IT Leader and an "individual contributor", eh?

Catmull believes that there are too few truly great leaders. These leaders have the ability to do a great job of listening to their team.

Additionally, while they are listening, they are trying to gain an understanding of just what kind of thinking has gone into the speaker's suggestion. Great leaders appreciate each and every contribution and in turn they feel free to use the best ideas no matter where they came from.

One of Pixar's breakthrough management techniques is that they use what they call a "brain trust" to solve problems. When a team gets itself in trouble (and we all do at some time or another), it can request the assembly of a brain trust.

A brain trust is a collection of Pixar's most creative people. The team with the problem presents their issues and then a two hour back and forth discussion ensues. During this discussion, there is no ego and nobody holds back on their comments / suggestions.

Through experimentation, Pixar has discovered that it is critical to NOT give the brain trust any authority over how the team solves its problems. This will screw up the dynamic of the brain trust session. Instead, make it a pure peer feedback session and watch the ideas flow…

It's from the forge of failure that the steel of success is formed.

Hard Work Does Not Guarantee Success, But Success Does Not Happen Without Hard Work.

- Dr. Jim Anderson

Create IT Departments That Are Productive And A Valuable Asset To The Rest Of The Company !

Dr. Jim Anderson is available to provide training and coaching on the topics that are the most important to people who have to manage IT departments: how can I build a productive IT department (and keep it together) while at the same time providing the rest of the company with the IT services that they need?

Dr. Anderson believes that in order to both learn and remember what he says, speakers need to laugh. Each one of his speeches is full of fun and humor so that what he says "sticks" with everyone.

Dr. Anderson's CIO SkillsTraining Includes:

1. How to identify and attract the right type of IT workers to your IT department.
2. How to build relationships with the company's senior management in order to get the support that you need?
3. How to stay on top of changing technology and security issues so that you never get surprised?

Dr. Jim Anderson works with over 100 customers per year. To invite Dr. Anderson to work with you, contact him at:

Phone: 813-418-6970 or
Email: jim@BlueElephantConsulting.com

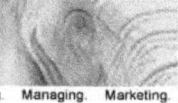

Photo Credits:

Cover - By: *sax
http://www.flickr.com/photos/saxonmoseley/

Chapter 1 - By: Austin & Zak
http://www.flickr.com/photos/zakh/

Chapter 2 - By: Kay Schlumpf
http://www.flickr.com/photos/princes_milady/

Chapter 3 - By: Troy B. Thompson
http://www.flickr.com/photos/troybthompson/

Chapter 4 - By: Fred Hasselman
http://www.flickr.com/photos/lost_archetype/

Chapter 5 - By: Preston Smalley
http://www.flickr.com/photos/prestons/

Chapter 6 - By: Joanna Sweeny
http://www.flickr.com/photos/josummers/

Chapter 7 - By: Alex Proimos
http://www.flickr.com/photos/proimos/

Chapter 8 - By: Andreas Nilsson
http://www.flickr.com/photos/andreasnilsson1976/

Chapter 9 - By: Bill Ohl
http://www.flickr.com/photos/haydnseek/

Chapter 10 - By: a n a n d h a m
http://www.flickr.com/photos/anandham/

Chapter 11 - By: Robert Morrison
http://www.flickr.com/photos/vortech/

Chapter 12 - By: TIG Photos
http://www.flickr.com/photos/theimagegroup/

Other Books By The Author

Product Management

- How To Have A Successful Product Manager Career: The Things That You Need To Be Doing TODAY In Order To Have A Successful Product Manager Career

- Product Manager Product Success: How to keep your product on track and make it become a success

- Communication Skills For Product Managers: The Communication Skills That Product Managers Need To Know How To Use In Order To Have A Successful Product

- Customer Lessons For Product Managers: Techniques For Product Managers To Better Understand What Their Customers Really Want

Public Speaking

- Secrets To Planning The Perfect Speech

- Secrets To Organizing The Perfect Speech: How to organize the best speech of your life!

- Secrets To Creating The Perfect Speech: How to create a speech that will make your message be remembered forever!

- How To Rehearse In Order To Give The Perfect Speech: How to effectively rehearse your next speech to that your message be remembered forever!

CIO Skills

- CIO Business Skills: How CIOs can work effectively with the rest of the company!

- Managing Your CIO Career: Steps That CIOs Have To Take In Order To Have A Long And Successful Career

- CIO Communication Skills Secrets: Tips And Techniques For CIOs To Use In Order To Become Better Communicators

- How CIOs Can Make Innovation Happen: Tips And Techniques For CIOs To Use In Order To Make Innovation Happen In Their IT Department

IT Manager Skills

- IT Manager Budgeting Skills

- IT Manager Career Secrets: Tips And Techniques That IT Managers Can Use In Order To Have A Successful Career

Negotiating

- Preparing For Your Next Negotiation: What You Need To Do BEFORE A Negotiation Starts In Order To Get The Best Possible Deal

- How To Open Your Next Negotiation: How To Start A Negotiation In Order To Get The Best Possible Outcome

Miscellaneous

- Power Distribution Unit (PDU) Secrets: What Everyone Who Works In A Data Center Needs To Know!

- Making The Jump: How To Land Your Dream Job When You Get Out Of College!

"Tips And Techniques That IT Managers Can Use In Order To Develop Leadership Skills"

This book has been written with one goal in mind – to show you how an IT manager can build needed leadership skills. It's not easy being an IT manager so we're going to show you what you need to be doing in order to not only manage your team, but to also be a leader to them!

Let's Make Your IT Career A Success!

What You'll Find Inside:

- **4 DRIVERS OF EMPLOYEE MOTIVATION THAT ALL IT LEADERS MUST KNOW**

- **IT LEADERS HAVE TWO OF THESE BUT DO THEY USE THEM?**

- **WHAT CAN COOL DESIGN FIRMS TEACH IT MANAGERS?**

- **IT MANAGER SECRETS FROM THE FOLKS AT PIXAR**

Dr. Jim Anderson brings his 25 years of real-world experience to this book. He's been an IT manager at some of the world's largest firms. He's going to show you what you need to do (and not do!) in order to successfully manage your career!

www.ingramcontent.com/pod-product-compliance
Lightning Source LLC
Chambersburg PA
CBHW071816170526
45167CB00003B/1333